On November 22, 2011 about noon, I sat on Delta airlines flight number 173 departing from John F. Kennedy international airport in New York to Ninoy Acquino international airport in Manila Philippines, via Narita, Tokyo. I was going to join 20 women leaders representing the Asia pacific women of faith network in a forum on restoring the dignity of women and girls by addressing violence against them.

The weather in New York was dull that day, leaving the world gloomy and teary. I stared blankly outside the misty window of the flight.

Then I heard a signal from my touch phone already in my bag under the seat in front of me. I had just received a new text message. I fumbled to get the phone from the handbag. Perhaps there was something urgent to respond to, before the flight takeoff.

It had been five years since I moved to New York with my family from my country Kenya, to take up a new position working for a non-profit organization to promote the leadership and empowerment of women and girls globally. The phone had become an extremely important tool of communicating with my children while I travelled, and with extended family members back home in Kenya on a regular basis.

The night before my travel, I had sent a text message to my mother in Kenya saying:

Mama, hope uko poa (mom, hope you are well). Do you remember when I was circumcised? What year? How about my two sister? How about you?

I am often astounded at my mom's memory. She could store so much information in her head, like a Mac book. At 67, my mom's memory was still the most reliable in our family. So my mom had responded to my message as surely as she always did.

I read the message, my heart warming up as the image of

my mom sitting on the maroon couch in our living room back home in the rural village in Igare, southwest Kenya came alive. My mom's text message read:

"U 1979, your sisters 1978, and me around 1952. Love u"

I texted back a quick *"thanks and luv u more"* in time before the crew ordered us to turn off all electronic devices in readiness for takeoff.

The takeoff was an arresting picture. The sound of the flight's wheels crushing on the tarmac on the runway was deafening. The flight's entire body trembled vividly, its wings flapping helplessly as it took off the ground, piercing unknowingly through the thick and gloomy clouds that bled with rain.

My mind escaped.

What makes Female Genital Cutting possible?

1952, 1978, 1979 and up to 2011: for 59 years, almost 6 decades (and beyond) Female Genital Cutting (FGC) has been possible, even inevitable for many girls from the Gusii ethnic community of Southwestern Kenya where I come from.

What makes FGC possible, even inevitable?

As I pondered this question, the following became apparent:

1). FGC embodies a web of cultural practices of the Gusii People:

FGC is not an end in itself.

It is embodies a whole web of cultural practices that have come to be valued as way of life of the Gusii ethnic community where I come from. FGC is only one component of the rituals undertaken as a rite of passage that form the cultural way of life for the Gusii. The entire rite of passage is, in fact, one of the most culturally- valued ways of being.

Over the years, this rite of passage has become a public routine practice that everyone looks up to; women, men, children, even priests and clan elders. Because girls are human beings, and their humanity is bound up in their society, they frequently yearn to partake in these activities, to be part of this culture and to belong.

The rite of passage in its entirety brings families together, and provides a social interactive forum for all, re-uniting and/or breaking families the way Thanksgiving holiday would do for Americans.

When I was growing up, FGC seemed inevitable, the natural thing for every girl to undergo, a stage in life that was exciting, albeit frightening. It had become part of the taken-for-granted norms and customs through which the life affairs of the Gusii people were conducted. We did not question it.

Sadly, these kinds of attitudes and belief systems continue to make FGC possible, even inevitable today.

We who practice FGC must stop claiming it is part of our culture, our traditional heritage to be proud of. As if even in human destruction, culture and tradition were to remain static and omnipotent. We must be open to understand why FGC must be eliminated, even when it has been part of our culture for centuries.

And we can stop FGC while still honoring our culture and tradition with a renewed rite of passage that does not harm.

We, together with those who are seeking to help must ask the following questions and let the communities affected answer them:

- How and why must FGC be understood as a practice that is harmful to girls, and to the entire community?

- Are there harmful practices surrounding male circumcision particularly in reproducing violent and highly sexualized masculinities? Why is it important to address the linkages between male circumcision and FGC?

- What opportunities are available for local communities to discuss the wider social system and way of life as it relates to the rite of passage that includes FGC?

- What would be viable alternative rites of passage, where needed, which would for example celebrate children and their growth, bring families together, and provide the space for education on values and life skills, emotional growth and bonding?

2). FGC is seen as an abnormal, barbaric practice of the

"uncivilized" tribes of Africa:

FGC is often presented as an abnormal, barbaric practice of uncivilized, archaic cultures of the African tribes.

It is indeed one of the most abhorred of the many so-called pathologies of Africa that has featured prominently in western cycles of advocacy and action.

This perception is wrong, because FGC is in fact not simply archaic - the practice has evolved, and continues to evolve, be it through medicalization, re-invention following the HIV and AIDS crisis or the recent movement toward alternative rites of passage.

FGC is also not a preserve of the illiterate; it also survives and even thrives among well educated communities, and has even been exported to diaspora communities living in so called developed continents of North America and Europe.

In fact I have even come to read that FGC was practiced in Europe and the United states as a treatment for hysteria.

FGC is not a uniform pathological cultural practice of the African peoples, because not all Africans practice it.

In Kenya alone where we have over 42 diverse ethnic communities and cultures, only a few groups such as the Gusii, Maasai, Turkana and Kuria practice FGC. And each of these groups has extremely diverse and distinct practices, rituals and degrees of cutting. Grouping all these practices together into one, which is often loathed among the international community, devalues African cultures and obscures the challenge of eradicating FGC.

FGC is not a practice of ignorance or barbarism. I have come to learn that some rituals that I considered barbaric such as bathing young girls in freezing water at 3 am in the morning or using stinging herbs on their bodies were intended to numb the body and serve as some form of anesthetics or sedatives. Remember this was done in a community that did not have access to modern medicine, or could not afford it. In fact women used traditional medicine to prevent bleeding. In recent years, the practice has been medicalized so that girls can actually undergo a medical procedure in hospital.

So it is not enough to be disgusted with FGC, or to present it as one of the 'pathologies' of the so-called 'Dark Continent, third world' of Africa.

It is not enough to want to 'save' girls who are at risk of FGC by uprooting them from their communities.

These measures may help. However, if they are not focused on combining urgent response with longer-term measures, they obscure hope, creativity and vision for lasting change. They undermine local leadership and agency. They do not tackle the root causes of the problem and its adverse effects. They may make FGC even more possible, albeit less publicly. And in extreme situations where communities want to defend even the most harmful of their cultures and preserve their perceived sense of worth, these measures do not offer alternative ways of being, and thus may exacerbate the problem, making FGC an inevitable identity marker for some.

In the case of my family, we were already considered non-persons because my parents did not bear sons. My mom did a great job through spiritual guidance, prayer and faith to teach us to have a sense of worth that was not given by society, but through God—who was neither male nor female. Had we not been circumcised, I wonder how much more humiliated and diminished my father and mom would have been made to feel in a community that overvalued boys and treated girls as if they were something less than whole.

For my mom, FGC was a combination of evils, not a real choice. FGC as a rite of passage provided the social space to wage the war against my mom (and father), a war against all families that bore only daughters.

The point here is to stress the need to go deeper to uncover the socio-political reality of FGC as a larger intractable affair of a community. Only then can we pinpoint the real challenges and find lasting solutions.

3). The links between FGC, male circumcision and gender inequality are seldom made:

FGC is not comparable to male circumcision, but it is inescapably linked to it among the Gusii. As part of a rite of passage, both FGC and male circumcision become strong identity markers for girls and boys, symbolically and/or substantively transforming childhood into adulthood, giving a sense of belonging based on age-sets.

Yet, male circumcision has never been perceived as a problem by most people opposed to FGC. In fact it is promoted as a healthy practice, and in recent years, even as an hygienic practice that could prevent HIV/AIDS infection. Male circumcision is widely practiced and highly medicalized even among western cultures.

Given that the circumcision of males and females is so intertwined in the process of social cohesion in the community, its acceptance makes it more difficult to oppose FGC.

Besides, although FGC has far worse implications for women's sexuality and biological wellbeing than male circumcision, addressing it must go beyond physical harm. It is important to address the psychological, socio-cultural, educational and other harms that surround both FGC and male circumcision.

With male circumcision in my culture comes a lot of pressure and expectation for young men to prove their virility or sexual prowess with young women. On the other hand, young women are encouraged to aspire to be good and meek wives, home keepers and above all to preserve their virginity. As circumcised girls are encouraged to remain virgins, circumcised boys are pressured to test their virility and manhood.

Hence, this is the foundation of other harmful cultural practices such as child marriage, or of sexual abuse, early pregnancy and rape. The seclusion period is a time for such training and education to take effect.

My mom took advantage of this space to provide us with alternative education, and to imbue in us visions for academic success and egalitarian relations with boys and men. But very few girls have such an opportunity.

Furthermore, male circumcision and FGC are embedded in a system of patriarchy that produces and reproduces inequality for boys and girls, women and men. It is the first stage in life where possession for boys and dispossession for girls occurs, and where kinship is bestowed upon boys as heirs.

Following circumcision in my village, the boys would move out of their 'mother's' house to a new home called *esaiga*. There are contemporary iterations of these gendered processes of discrimination and inequality in urban settings where boys may not move out, but would have a separate bedroom, physically far away from the mom's, or would move to the 'servant's quarter' in a city home. The understanding is that, in this new home, the boys would learn to be independent, be sexually virile and tend to 'manly' chores. The boys would no longer be expected to do household chores such as drawing water or cooking.

The gender roles become much more marked at this stage, and it becomes almost a taboo for boys to enter the kitchen. The boys would be encouraged to sit with men, and often would be served meals by their mothers or sisters. Older boys would soon marry and move to a section of land allocated to them. The girls would be disposed of their right to inherit property as they were considered 'temporary' and not part of the kinship system.

So, besides the physical harm, FGC sustains discriminatory socio-cultural systems and provides the stage for inequality between women and men, boys and girls to be enacted and lived. Ending it would be a serious political process that is highly contested among those who want to keep the status quo and marginal position of women and girls.

4). The politics of charity oversimplify both the problem and solutions:

FGC is the kind of practice that causes donors to want to act quickly to alleviate suffering. Having served in the international non-profit development sector for over a decade now, I have observed some of the ways that the emotions of fear, shock, anger and revulsion are expressed by westerners who encounter this practice: 'I am so fortunate that I was not born in such a culture,' or 'how could someone do that‖ or 'it is absolutely disgusting' or 'it is because of illiteracy' or 'we must stop this madness.'

With such comments, I have often given in; feeling that, by sharing my story, I would put myself and my culture on trial. And who am I anyway, to tell such 'powerful' people what was possible, what people affected or at risk could do themselves, and how they could support them? There are various projects and programs that have emerged out of such pain, disgust and often-genuine desire to help eradicate FGC, from documentaries, to rescue centers, to asylums, to campaigns, to trainings, to advocacy; and the list goes on.

When donors and other individuals of good will allow such assumptions to motivate their action, they alienate and distance themselves from the survivors and practitioners of FGC whom they perceive to be unlike themselves. They remain ignorant, distracted and dangerously consumed by their power over African women whom they consider aberrant and helpless. This serves many purposes, key among them to silence those affected in ways that continue to suppress awareness. It also excludes entire communities from the path to find solutions to their own problems without feeling judged, diminished and denigrated.

Such an approach demands quick fixes, insisting that projects be created and finished quickly, rather than following projects whenever they lead with attention to accountability and long-term social change. It obscures the challenges of patriarchy, limiting it to what is considered 'savage and violent African cultures.'

This makes it difficult to break down the structures of patriarchy and where necessary draw parallels with western cultures, where the pressure to have women and girls sexually desirable has led to all kinds of 'mutilations' of women's bodies. This is not to say that such 'mutilations' are the same, but that they share a common system of patriarchy that makes all of these practices of oppression possible and inevitable. When this is understood, the common goal would be one of solidarity across cultures, with increased cultural competence to break down the structures of patriarchy forever.

In responding to FGC, it is more important to focus on the depth of the approach and the measurement of success, rather than resorting to quick fixes and sheer numbers.

There are many wonderful and successful program approaches that have achieved a great deal in the field of eradicating FGC. Such programs have been systematic, open-ended and community-led. They don't presume that local people have all the knowledge, critical perspective or answers, but that they are the bearers of possibility.

These approaches are grounded on an understanding that FGC is multi-dimensional; therefore ending it is a process of empowerment and social change.

5). The law alone may not eliminate FGC:

My country Kenya has worked hard to finally prohibit FGC by law. In October 2011, the Kenyan Prohibition of Female Genital Mutilation (FGC) Act No. 32 was signed into law, criminalizing FGC. It also prohibits its practices including the use of derogatory language for those who have not undergone the practice.

The law is undoubtedly a powerful tool, and huge step towards bringing an end to this practice. I am not sure how many people have been prosecuted following this law. What I am sure of is that the practice continues, albeit more privately, among many in my community.

There are a number of efforts by the government and civil society actors to increase knowledge and awareness about this law. The challenge is to counter the power of the social norms and practices that not only perpetuate FGC but also those that make it possible.

The law does not offer alternatives to the entrenched forms of meaning that come with the act of FGC. Its implementation is also a challenge given that women's access to the justice system is often prohibitively expensive and difficult to navigate. The law is necessary but cannot be efficient by itself.

Ending FGC is possible, forever

Yes, I am convinced that ending FGC is possible, across generations and forever. The challenges highlighted above need to be addressed.

Within the absence of choice to circumcise my sisters and me, my mom found a creative opportunity to challenge and destabilize the social order of circumcision. She moderated its various harmful effects and provided us with an alternative education and awareness. She empowered us and herself, refusing to reproduce the inequalities that circumcision intended to breed. She never once devalued our sexual power, nor intended for us to be married off.

Mom offered us a whole range of opportunities in a social setting that had limited choices for girls.

Circumcision was made possible and even inevitable for my sisters, my mom and me. It has been made possible for millions of women and girls for centuries. Few have been able to break the silence and share their own experiences in their own voice.

Circumcision is inevitably part of my identity. It does not hold me back from being fully human; Because I know, just as my mom, sisters and other women know, how to transform its negative effects and get to the finish line.

Today, we have upset the structures of patriarchy and inequality that make FGC possible in ways that cannot be reversed. In my entire extended family, circumcision is no longer an indicator of what it means to be human.

I am so proud that my daughter and son are not circumcised, and yet they are considered fully human and equally valued in my village and community in Kisii, Kenya. All of my adult and teenage nieces are not circumcised, and they have achieved a great deal in their social and academic lives.

We are sure that with this generation, FGC has finally been put to a halt. By extension, the success is being modeled, re-humanizing those of us who have undergone it as survivors more than victims, and proving that eradicating FGC is in fact possible. One can find empowering stories of this kind where the struggle has been won in my village and beyond.

Ending FGC is not a dream, a pathological wish, or helpless endeavor. It is a reality to be achieved.

We have come a long way, and I have no doubt that, eventually, we are going to succeed in our struggle to the point that FGC is no longer possible or inevitable.

The sad thing is that there are girls today who are still undergoing FGC.

And with globalization and its culture of consumerism, new forms of socio-technological structures have emerged that are being misused in ways that rob girls and young women of their clitoris, albeit not by FGC. These modern structures exploit girls (and boys) through human trafficking, internet-based sexual exploitation, cyber prostitution and pornography, commercialization and sexualization of their bodies, sex tourism and violent video games among other practices.

With these practices, one can find young women (and men), whose clitoris (or penises) are exploited, brutalized, overused and misused in modern societies across the world.

We need to win the struggle today for these girls and boys, women and men, facing these threats to human dignity and wellbeing.

This is an excerpt of the book titled:

Pervasive Violence: What Makes Female Genital Cutting Possible, Even Inevitable?

By Jackie Ogega

Published on Amazon

December 2012